D1504506

EXERCISE
GUIDE
TO
BETTER
GOLF

Other Champion Press titles include:
* *Play Ball! The Official Little League Fitness Guide*
* *Shoulder & Arm Exercises for Athletes*

To order more copies of this book or Champion Press titles listed above, please call (310) 419-8669.

EXERCISE GUIDE TO BETTER GOLF

A Scientifically Based Exercise Program for Golfers!

Researched and tested by
Centinela Hospital Medical Center
Official Hospital of the PGA TOUR
and Senior PGA TOUR

Endorsed by the PGA TOUR
and Senior PGA TOUR

Developed by:

- Frank W. Jobe, M.D.
  *Orthopaedic Consultant to the PGA TOUR
  and Senior PGA TOUR*

- Lewis A. Yocum, M.D.
  *Orthopaedic Consultant to the PGA TOUR
  and Senior PGA TOUR*

- Robert E. Mottram, PT, ATC
  *Senior Physical Therapist and Athletic Trainer of
  the PGA TOUR and Senior PGA TOUR*

- Marilyn M. Pink, MS, PT
  *Director/Assistant Administrator
  Centinela Hospital Biomechanics Laboratory*

Champion Press
Inglewood, California

Copyright 1994 Centinela Hospital Medical Center
All rights reserved including the right of reproduction in whole
or in part in any form.

Published by Champion Press
Centinela Hospital Medical Center
555 E. Hardy Street
Inglewood, California 90301

Champion Press is a registered trademark of Centinela
Hospital Medical Center

Manufactured in the United States of America

Library of Congress Cataloging-in-Publication-Data

Jobe, Frank W., 1925-
Yocum, Lewis A., 1947-
Mottram, Robert E., 1952-
Pink, Marilyn M., 1953-
Exercise Guide to Better Golf.

1. Golf-Training   2. Exercise
I. Jobe, Frank W.   II. Centinela Hospital Medical Center
GV979.E9E94   1994   613.7'11-dc20   CIP
ISBN 0-93-669106-9

Exercise Guide To Better Golf
Scientifically and Professionally designed for all Golfers!

Researched and tested by Centinela Hospital Medical Center,
Official Hospital of the PGA TOUR

Developed in conjunction with the PGA TOUR and Senior
PGA TOUR

Developed by Frank W. Jobe, M.D.; Lewis A. Yocum, M.D.;
Robert E. Mottram, PT, ATC; and Marilyn M. Pink, MS, PT

PREFACE BY
TOM KITE
AND
DAVE STOCKTON

Tom Kite

Ten years ago, who would have thought you would be reading a fitness book designed especially to improve your golf game. Back then, the relationship between physical conditioning and better golf didn't rank high in the minds of most players. There were some players on TOUR that would run and do some stretching by themselves, but most players did not exercise. We knew that strength, flexibility and endurance were important in sports, but golf was considered, by many, as a "nonathletic" sport. The feeling was that if you wanted to lower your handicap, you would take lessons and spend more time on the driving range and putting green. Many of us did not understand the importance of conditioning and fitness for our profession.

Well, now we know better, thanks in large part to the pioneering efforts of Centinela Hospital Medical Center and a new generation of pro golfers — men and women alike — who understand the importance of physical fitness. This unique book offers a golf specific exercise program which lays out a comprehensive program which any golfer can follow to lower the risk of injury, increase their enjoyment of the game, and possibly improve their performance.

I had the good fortune of being a test subject in Centinela Hospital's biomechanics laboratory research project in 1984. Their ongoing study on the golf swing began in 1983 by analyzing the swings of professional golfers. Centinela's medical experts used this information to devise this exercise program to stretch and strengthen the muscles specifically used in golf. I'm sure you'll enjoy the book as much as I do.

Dave Stockton

When I came out on the Senior PGA TOUR in 1992, I thought I'd see a bunch of old, broken down bodies. I figured I'd be one of the few guys working out and staying in shape. But that is not the way it is at all. These guys know how valuable it is to stay injury free and in good shape. There is too much at stake to not be in top physical condition. When I started playing golf, it was thought that nothing mattered in golf except hitting golf balls. Modern research has changed all of that. I wish I had done this exercising all my life.

Fortunately, players like Floyd, Charles, Hill, Player, Colbert, Weiskopf, Archer, Gieberger, myself and others, have a wonderful place to exercise and receive treatment while on the road. The place — the Centinela Hospital Player Fitness Center. These vans are a combination of an athletic training room, sports medicine clinic, and gymnasium, and are very valuable to the pro golfers. In fact the TOUR surveyed its members on a range of subjects and asked what they thought was the most important program offered by the TOUR. That particular question was a multiple choice. Among the possibilities: rules seminars, media services, course conditioning, the pension plan, day care services, and statistic services. The Centinela Hospital Player Fitness Center was a walkaway winner. There have been many times when players who would have had to withdraw from a tournament, were instead, able to receive treatment in the Fitness Center and continue playing. In fact a couple of us have gone on to win during a questionable week. Even if the Fitness Center doesn't make us win a tournament, they make it so we can play. And that is so important out here. We don't have a disabled list. If you don't play, there's no pay. The Centinela Hospital Player Fitness Center also offers a relaxing place to meet at the golf course. We can either put ourselves through a tough workout, or simply visit with the guys in a congenial environment.

EXERCISE GUIDE TO BETTER GOLF

CHAPTER ONE

THE BACKGROUND FOR THIS BOOK

The Background For This Book

Since early 1985 Centinela Hospital Medical Center has been working with the PGA TOUR to promote the health, fitness and performance of the players as they travel around the country.

This book stems from our day-to-day involvement  with the pros, coupled with Centinela's ongoing biomechanics research into the golf swing and years of experience in sports medicine. The result is a unique exercise program tailored to golfers - beginners and club champs alike - with specific exercise routines to help stretch and strengthen the muscle groups most involved in the golf swing. Stick with this program - before you tee off and between rounds - and you can expect the following benefits.

- Greater flexibility and mobility in your swing.
- Improved muscle endurance, which will pay off on the back nine, especially during hot weather and on long or hilly courses.
- Enhanced body tone and weight maintenance.
- Fewer aches and pains after a demanding day on the course and, in the long term, a more conditioned body that is less prone to injuries.
- An increased enjoyment of the game.

We are convinced that walking 18 holes and spending time on the driving range is not enough to keep golfing muscles in top shape and minimize the risk of injury. While some golfers think overall fitness is not critical to success as in most other sports, our book reflects a growing appreciation for golf's many physical challenges. Out-of-shape golfers can still enjoy the game, but it takes relatively strong and flexible golfing muscles to play it well, make improvements, and avoid common injuries.

If you are pursuing a lower handicap, it might seem more productive to work on your swing instead of our golf-specific exercise program. But we are learning through Centinela Hospital's biomechanics research and experience on the pro tours, that improved fitness underscores a more enjoyable and healthier game. In fact, we hope all golfers will appreciate the natural marriage between fitness and golf instruction.

Renowned instructor Bob Toski once said, "You can't shape a golf swing if you're not in shape." And he is right.

The Centinela Hospital Biomechanics Laboratory Research

How do we know the exercises in this book will help your golf game?

Much of our advice has evolved from ongoing research at the Centinela Hospital Biomechanics Laboratory. Since 1983, we have been testing professional golfers to evaluate the golf swing.

Centinela researchers began studying minute details of the golf swing by gathering data from high-speed cameras, electromyography (EMG) and computers. Based on these studies, we have isolated the muscle groups most prominent in the backswing and the downswing, at impact, and in the follow-through. Among our findings:

1. A good golf swing uses the left side of the body as much as the right.

The golf swing is a balanced activity; the net muscular output on the left side and the right side is equal. However, many instructors and golfers still emphasize the left side, arguing that it provides the power for a right-handed golfer. Our studies of the shoulder and hips have shown that the right side is at least as active as the left. The exercises in this book reflect this research by giving equal emphasis to both sides of the body.

2. The hips initiate movement into the ball.

One of the questions we wanted to answer was "what part of the body initiates the swing?" It is clear from our data that the hip muscles become active before the upper body turns into the shot. Each specific muscle of the hip has a unique function. These muscles fire in a precise sequence which initiates the motion of the golf swing.

3. The body acts like a whip during the golf swing.

One of the most frequently asked questions is "where does the power come from?" The golfer's definition of power has to do with the 'umpf' with which one hits the ball. So, where does the 'umpf' come from? It comes from a synchronous coordination of precise muscle firing throughout the swing. The body acts like a whip during the golf swing. The feet pushing against the ground cause a ground reaction force which sequentially travels up through the hips, the trunk and finally out the arms. The energy gains momentum as it travels through the whip. The arms and trunk play a small role in adding "power" to the swing, but more importantly they are an integral part of the coordinated sequence. If the sequence is disturbed at any point of the swing  (or whip), the momentum and power are dissipated throughout the body. The only choice the body has is to substitute and try again to initiate the 'power' after the point of disruption. Invariably this puts the golfer at risk for injury.

4. Trunk rotation and flexibility are especially important.

The most noticeable difference between pros and amateurs is in trunk rotation. Older and less skilled players tend to use less than half the trunk rotation of a younger or more skilled player. This lack of flexibility and strength explains why ability decreases with age. Golfers gradually lose the arc of motion that enables the body to transmit maximum velocity to the clubhead at impact.

When you don't adequately use the trunk muscles, you must compensate for the lack of sufficient rotation to attain optimal clubhead speed at impact. Unfortunately, simply "muscling" the ball to increase clubhead speed causes you to swing too fast and puts added stress on your muscles and joints. As the rounds progress, the muscles become increasingly prone to fatigue and injury.

5. The scapular muscles and rotator cuff muscles are crucial in the golf swing.

Many injuries of the shoulder area in the golfer can be traced to problems in these two groups of muscles. These muscles help to precisely position the upper extremity and hence prevent injury. The rotator cuff muscles are very active in the swing, and are vulnerable to overuse and microtrauma. The scapular muscles play an important role by stabilizing the scapula, allowing the arms to function properly.

6. Skilled players are more efficient at using their muscles.

Our research has shown that skilled golfers are extremely efficient at using all their muscles when swinging the club. The pros studied use a far lower percentage of their maximum muscular output potential as they swing, compared to the amateurs tested. And, we all know what will make you a skilled player ... practice, practice, practice.

7. Men and women utilize the same muscle firing patterns.

Our data shows that men and women utilize the same muscles. The timing and the intensity relative to overall strength of the muscle firing is exactly the same. Based upon this information, instructional techniques and exercise programs can be the same for the two groups.

The PGA TOUR and Senior PGA TOUR Connection

Research is never an end unto itself. The biomechanics research done at Centinela Hospital helped to further injury prevention and rehabilitation for the golfer. As this work came to the public eye, Dr. Frank Jobe (the medical director of Centinela's Biomechanics research lab) was asked to be the Orthopaedic Consultant for the PGA TOUR and the Senior PGA TOUR. From that connection, Centinela Hospital then began to provide Player Fitness Centers for each of the Tours.

The Centinela Hospital Player Fitness Centers are 36-foot long by 24-foot wide trucks which are driven to the different tournament sites. Once the truck arrives at the site, it hydraulically expands to a 500-square foot fitness and rehabilitation center. It contains the latest exercise and therapeutic intervention equipment, and is staffed by two professional physical therapists under the medical direction of Dr. Frank Jobe and Dr. Lewis Yocum.

Hence, the exercises in this book come not from an isolated ivory tower of research; but rather from an intimate connection between research and clinical practice. The professional golfers note the value of such a connection as they see their improved flexibility, strength and endurance result in greater individual success on the tour. Long hitting player JC Snead says, "The value of keeping your muscles toned is similar to that of a new, fresh rubber band versus that of an old stale rubber band. Like a new rubber band, stronger muscles will stretch further and contract faster if they're toned, unlike muscles that are weak and stiff."

CHAPTER TWO

HOW TO USE THIS BOOK

How To Use This Book

We have created a comprehensive exercise program that includes two routines: Program A (Chapter 3) and Program B (Chapter 4). Each exercise routine encompasses both stretching and strengthening. The improved flexibility and body tone will prepare you for a better and safer round of golf.

All recommended exercises are relatively easy to learn and perform. In this book there are pictorial exercise cards which you can tear out and keep near your workout station. The only equipment you will require is a pair of adjustable dumbbells. Each program takes 25 to 30 minutes.

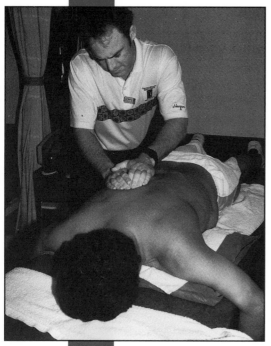

To work out each part of your body, and to add variety to your exercise sessions, we recommend you alternate the two routines. This will also allow specific muscle groups time to recover between workouts.

We encourage you to work a stretching and strengthening routine into your schedule six days a week. When these exercises are performed consistently, the body adjusts to the constant stretching and strengthening repetitions. Conversely, it ignores or resists the once- or twice-a-week exercise session. Consistency is all important. Your body will respond much better to a regular routine rather than doing all the exercises on a sporadic basis.

Prior to beginning a round of golf, it is important to warm up and stretch (Chapter 5). This temporarily increases your heartrate and helps to make you limber for the first drive.

Cardiovascular conditioning (Chapter 6) is the other component for a well-planned golf exercise program. Endurance for golfers can make a difference, especially in the older player. "The difference is that I feel I'm playing as well as I once did, except it's harder to play day in and day out," says Al Gieberger, "In other words, endurance makes a difference. With my cardiovascular training program, I can consistently play multiple days in a row."

Raymond Floyd, playing in his fourth decade on the TOUR, credits much of his current success to his daily exercise program. "At my age," he says, "it's tougher to keep up with the younger guys and with my hectic travel schedule. I can really tell the difference when I don't do my stretches, especially as I get older. The body doesn't heal as fast, so I try to stretch and work out every day, even when I can't get out and hit the ball."

We have pinpointed the areas in which golfers need help, so you can be confident that our overall exercise program will result in greater strength and flexibility. Since we all respond at different rates, progress will depend on your current fitness level, your faithfulness in following the prescribed exercises, your level of intensity and your body's physiology. Whatever your level, if you stick to this program you should begin to notice improvements in two to three weeks. More noticeable changes in your physique, such as improved body tone, will take three months or longer, depending on your commitment.

While this is a "sport-specific" exercise book, many of these golf exercises will also help you improve your overall fitness level which may be helpful in other sports and daily activities.

Stretching Guidelines

If you tend to be a slow starter in golf, chances are you don't warm up and stretch beforehand, forcing your body to perform with an added handicap.

Muscles that are warm and stretched prior to teeing off are supple and loose, enabling your body to perform to its full potential. Simply knowing that you are warmed up and physically ready to play also gives you greater mental confidence.

The improved flexibility you gain from stretching will increase your range of motion and improve your ability to have a complete backswing and extended follow-through. Stretching helps your muscles work at their optimal length or tension. By elongating the tissue around the joints, you give the joints greater range of motion.

Golfers on the professional tour have a tendency to be tight in the flexors and extensors of their legs and hips. In contrast, their rotational movements in their hips and trunk demonstrate good range of motion. Because the golf swing involves full hip and trunk turns, it is easy to understand why their joints rotate well. The swing does not however, require a lot of flexing and extending, therefore the low back, as well as the front and back of the legs and hips may become tight.

"Flexibility gives you a little extra turn as you swing," noted PGA TOUR pro, Tom Kite. This allows you to incorporate the body's big muscles as you rotate into the shot, with your arms and hands following through as you release.

Proper warm-up also helps prevent injury and nagging pain by stretching those parts of the body involved in the golf swing. Muscles and surrounding tissue tend to shorten with time unless stretched on a regular basis. When slightly elongated, they work more efficiently and with less risk of strain or tears. As the body ages, it needs help to retain its full range of motion. Otherwise the connecting tissues - ligaments, tendons and muscles - will shorten in time.

"It is my impression that one of the most important parts of a golfers fitness, especially as they grow older, is their flexibility," reports Bruce Crampton. "Keeping joints and muscles supple is what allows one to make a proper move away from the ball, and then return all the way through to the finish. If the golfer is tight, he or she may have a tendency to hurry their swing because of the short turn. Injury prevention is important to me too, therefore keeping flexible will lessen the chance of straining my muscles and joints."

Stretching only before you play is not enough. Ideally, you should stretch daily so you retain a wide range of motion in all the major muscle groups from your neck to your calves.

Our suggested home stretches are designed to take advantage of floor space, privacy and available time. You can relax as you stretch, lingering on your favorite stretches without feeling rushed.

By doing the flexibility routines on a regular basis, the various stretches will become familiar and easy to execute. Once you are able to do them from memory, you can incorporate them into your daily routine whether you are at home, a health club, the workplace or the golf course.

A few guidelines to consider when you begin your stretches are as follows:

1. Ideally, you should warm up before starting your flexibility routine or putting your hands on a club. This means raising your body temperature by walking briskly for several minutes, running in place, jogging slowly, or doing a few jumping jacks. This literally "warms up" the body by increasing tissue temperature, which makes nerve impulses travel faster, and leads to more efficient performance. A rise in body temperature also promotes muscle flexibility by loosening the connective tissue and improving the joint lubrication mechanisms. This way you are less likely to pull or strain soft tissue.

2. Gently stretch a muscle through the desired range of motion and hold the limb at the end of the range for 10 to 15 seconds. This is better than doing bounce-type stretches. When you bounce while stretching, your momentum is harder to stop, the muscles shorten and there is a higher risk of injury. Equally important, you prevent the tissues from elongating effectively. This is somewhat similar to pulling on salt water taffy. If you were to pull hard and fast on the taffy, it would not move. However, with a long and slow pull, the taffy would gradually stretch and lengthen. When you concentrate on slow, steady stretching, the muscles are forced to do the work. This kind of "static" stretching also provides better feedback from the ligaments and tendons, allowing them to alert you if you are pushing too far.

3. Do each stretching exercise carefully, avoiding the initial tendency to rush or reach too far. Move slowly and deliberately through the indicated range of motion, then gradually try to increase the range as your flexibility increases.

4. We believe in a "no strain, no pain" approach, especially if certain stretches feel too strenuous or if you are limited by arthritis in your joints. Comfort is the key. If you are hurting, you will likely experience a reflexive muscle tightening as the muscles protect themselves from a potentially damaging motion.

5. Repeat each stretch two times. And remember, golf is a bilateral game. Do an equal number of repetitions on each side of the body. This keeps your muscles evenly balanced.

6. Occasionally, do these stretches in front of a mirror for accurate visual feedback. When you see yourself stretching, you can better recognize if you are doing it as pictured in the book.

7. Do not be discouraged in the beginning if your body is so inflexible that you have difficulty stretching very far without some discomfort. Your body will gradually yield as your flexibility improves. In time, you will find that it takes less effort to attain the same degree of stretch.

While the 12 stretching exercises focus on the important joints and muscles used in the golf swing, they will also improve your overall flexibility for everyday activities. By doing these stretches you address your neck, shoulders, chest, upper and lower back muscles, as well as your hips and upper and lower leg muscles.

Strengthening Guidelines

Striking a golf ball accurately and aggressively over 18 holes requires strength and muscle endurance. Traditionalists advocate hitting buckets of balls on  the driving range and playing a lot of golf to develop these skills. We believe it takes a conscientious effort to strengthen the golfing muscles through an exercise and weight training program - one that will also be a safeguard against injury.

With a proper golf swing, you can hit a golf ball relatively far regardless of your size. Improving your distance requires a combination of several factors — technique, flexibility and strength. Hitting hundreds of balls on the driving range is simply not enough. Hitting power is derived from the speed of your golf club at impact, which comes primarily from strengthening all the muscles that help generate that power — the legs, hips, shoulders, upper body and arms.

For years most professional golfers hesitated to commit themselves to specific weight training programs, believing they would hurt their golf swing by developing large, tight muscles. This is simply not true. By combining a strengthening routine with stretching exercises every day, you will become increasingly flexible, not "muscle tight."

On the professional golf tours, many players have discovered that working with weights benefits their golf swing, provided they train on a regular basis. Many golfers who come regularly into the Centinela Hospital Player Fitness Center report greater body control as they swing, enabling them to strike the ball more accurately and consistently throughout the round. This enables them to swing the club more efficiently and conserve energy as a round progresses. Increased endurance also helps them to play at their peak for a longer period, since they are not as tired.

Finally, well-conditioned muscles recover faster and are less prone to injury. This strengthening program will help you avoid sore muscles, nagging aches and pains, and injury that can inhibit your golf game, especially as you get older. "My strengthening program is done in order to keep me from injuring myself," says 1991 Senior TOUR leading money winner Mike Hill. "When I'm stronger I also feel more solid through the swing."

A few guidelines to consider when you begin your strengthening exercises are as follows:

1. Prepare your body for each workout by starting with a brief warm-up session (three to five minutes) that includes light aerobics (e.g., running in place, a brisk walk, jumping jacks or jumping rope) and several stretches.

2. When using weights and doing repetitions, consider your own strength and condition, and start conservatively. Since you will develop muscle strength gradually with your program, begin with a minimal amount of weight, using comfort as your barometer. The exercises herein are for both the large, powerhouse muscles and for some of the smaller, fine tuning muscles. Thus, the amount of weight you choose for the different exercises will vary. In selecting the right weight, you should be able to do 10 repetitions and feel it while being comfortable.

3. When you start, do each exercise slowly in a set

of 10 repetitions. Week two, add a second set of 10 repetitions, then a third set the following week.

4. For each exercise, build up to '3 sets of 10 reps.' That means to do the exercise 10 times, rest 1 minute, repeat the exercise 10 times, rest and repeat another 10 times. Once you can do a given weight for 3 sets of 10 reps, it is time to increase the weight.

We recommend you make small weight increases more frequently, rather than waiting longer periods and making larger ones. If you need more resistance with exercises that don't require weights, simply hold the muscle contraction longer.

5. Whatever your starting point, extreme soreness the following day indicates you probably did too much. Continue doing six workouts a week, but lessen the intensity and gradually work your way up. Don't be alarmed if you experience some minor muscle soreness, usually related to the newness of the exercise program. It should subside within a day or two.

6. Take your time as you do these exercises, allowing a 30 second rest between sets, and one minute between individual exercises. This allows the muscles to recover.

7. Our program will strengthen both sides of the body during every workout. These exercises work the front and back of the body as well as the right and left sides, helping you avoid long-range problems that can occur with unbalanced strengthening regimens.

8. While we have designed an easy home workout program that does not require sophisticated weight-training equipment, for maximum benefit you should still obtain some inexpensive hand-weights to provide the necessary muscle resistance. Get

adjustable dumbbells instead of fixed-weight dumbbells so you can add weight in one, two or three half-pound increments.

9. We stress the importance of quality over quantity. Be deliberate in your exercises. Concentrate on the movement and body parts involved, rather than simply going through the motions. Remember, in exercise as with golf, "speed kills."

10. Keep an exercise "flow sheet," listing each exercise and noting the date you started, the repetitions, sets and any weights involved. This way you can objectively chart your progress.

Cautionary Notes

If you have had any medical problems, such as high blood pressure or heart ailments, consult your physician before undertaking any exercise program. Furthermore:

1. Listen to your body and be careful not to overstrain. If you are experiencing undue pain, discomfort or exhaustion, stop and ask your physician's advice.

2. If you are having difficulty or discomfort, your program may need to be modified, taking into account arthritis, lower-back pain or other restrictive conditions. Again your doctor will be your best guide.

3. Older individuals should avoid excessive strain, since this could damage weak vertebrae, particularly in women who may be developing osteoporosis.

CHAPTER THREE

PROGRAM A

Flexibility Program A

1. Neck Rotation

2. Posterior Shoulder Stretch

3. Chest Stretch

4. Trunk Forward Flexion

5. Trunk Rotation

6. Trunk Side Bend Stretch

1. Neck Rotation

This exercise simulates the actual neck movements in a good golf swing - chin to shoulder on the backswing and chin to shoulder on the follow-through.

Stand upright with your body facing straight forward, then look as far around as you can over the right shoulder (but don't cheat by turning your shoulders). Take your left hand and gently push against the chin in the same direction. Hold for a 10 - 15 count and repeat, then switch sides. Looking as far over your left shoulder as you can, push your chin to the left side with your right hand, hold and repeat.

Dave Stockton

Brad Fabel

2. Posterior Shoulder Stretch

This stretch increases flexibility in the back portion of your shoulder (the rotator cuff and joint capsule), which is involved on your left side during the back-swing (if you are right-handed) and on the right side as you rotate through the shot and into your finish.

Standing erect, reach across your body and grasp the back of your elbow with the opposite hand. Pull that arm across your body and under your chin, as far back as you can. Hold and repeat with both arms.

We cannot overemphasize the importance of this exercise, as the rotator cuff muscles are especially vulnerable to injury over time.

3. Chest Stretch

This exercise will loosen your chest muscles, helping you gain and retain your desired range of motion as you swing. Remember, you are often in a position where your shoulders are rounded forward and your hands are out in front (e.g., the address position and the swing itself). So if your chest muscles are tight, your upper body movement is limited.

This exercise can be done either while standing or sitting. While maintaining an erect trunk posture, clasp hands behind your back raise your arms up and out. Retract your elbows and shoulder blades backwards, as if you were sticking your chest out. Inhale to increase the stretch in your chest muscles.

Bob Charles

4. Trunk Forward Flexion

This single exercise will prepare you for a safer round of golf by effectively stretching your hamstrings, lower back, and the extensors in your buttocks.

Stand erect, feet flat on the ground. Gently bend forward at the waist until you are able to grasp your ankles, bending your knees as necessary. Let your neck and arms relax as you bend forward slowly from the hips. Holding your ankles, straighten your knees until you feel a comfortable stretch in the back of your legs. Hold for 10 - 15 seconds. As you return to a standing position be sure to bend your knees as you straighten your trunk.

Larry Mize

5. Trunk Rotation

This easy stretch works the sides of the abdomen and the trunk rotators (the small and deep muscles that parallel the spine). To get an excellent spine stretch, do this exercise sitting down, as the pelvis will remain stationary. Rotate your upper body around so that you grab the back of the bench or chair.

Bruce Crampton

Try to look over your shoulder as you stretch. Increase the tension in your stretch by pulling yourself around a little farther with your hands. This gently increases the effectiveness of the stretch. Hold for 10 - 15 seconds and repeat. Do this to both sides.

If you are standing, simply back up against a tree or any fixed object. Rotate your upper body and grab onto the fixed object without moving your feet. Try to look over your shoulder as you twist. Then increase the tension in your stretch by pulling yourself around a little further with both hands. This gently increases the effectiveness of the stretch. Hold for 10 - 15 seconds and repeat.

6. Trunk Side Bend Stretch

Since a golf swing requires a combination of horizontal rotation and side bending, the following exercise will improve your lateral flexibility and reduce the risk of strains in your rib cage and trunk.

Stand with your feet shoulder width apart and your right arm elevated over your head. Lean directly to your left side so that you may place your left hand on or close to the side of your lower thigh or knee.

You may actually support some body weight with your hand. Continue the lean so that you feel a comfortable stretch along the right side of your trunk. Hold this position for 10 to 15 seconds and repeat. Repeat the exercise on the other side.

Jim McGovern

Strengthening Program A

1. Countertop Push-ups with a Plus

2. Bent-over Row

3. Shoulder Extension

4. Shoulder External Rotation

5. Shoulder Internal Rotation

6. Shoulder Abduction/Flexion/ Internal Rotation

Fred Funk

1. Countertop Push-ups with a Plus

Tried and true push-ups are a convenient and effective way to strengthen muscles that are important in the golf swing: the pectoral muscles (chest), the anterior deltoid (front of the shoulder) the serratus anterior (the shoulder blade), and the triceps (back of the arms). Our research has shown how important the "pecs" are in carrying the arms forward during the swing, by adding power and control of the club. Since many people lack sufficient upper body strength, push-ups aid these power muscles, which in turn help sustain a more effective swing.

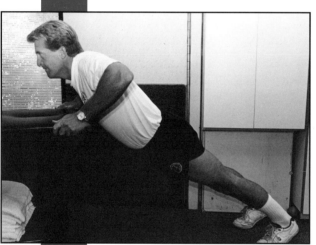

Using a waist-high countertop, place your hands a little wider than shoulder width apart and position yourself so your arms are at a 90 degree angle from your body. Slowly lower yourself until your chest comes within a few inches from the edge of the counter, then push back to the starting position. Make sure you push yourself up as far as you can go so that you feel your shoulder blades separate on your back. Stay on the balls of your feet and keep your body straight (locking your body so your stomach and back do not sag). Make sure your arms and chest do all the work.

2. Bent-over Row

This exercise strengthens several specific muscle groups, including the area between the shoulder blades.

Bill Glasson

While standing with your feet fairly wide apart and knees slightly bent, bend forward at the waist and rest your head on a table or countertop so you have good balance and can avoid lower back strain. Resting your head helps ensure that your upper body remains stationary and your shoulders and arms do all the work. The legs should be spread wide enough and comfortably bent so that you have three "support points," placing little strain on your back.

Your arms should hang in front of you. Hold a weight in each hand. Bend your elbows as you lift the weights towards the ceiling.

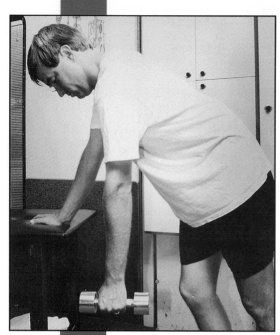

Davis Love III

3. Shoulder Extension

To work the latissimus dorsi muscle (located across your back and at your side), bend over as shown in the photograph and rest the non-involved hand on a low countertop or any flat surface for support. With your arm extended, pull the weight back to a parallel position with the floor. Hold for a one-count before slowly lowering the weight to the starting position.

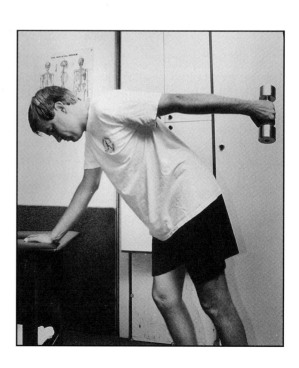

4. Shoulder External Rotation

Our studies have shown that the shoulder's rotator cuff muscles are highly active in the golf swing. These muscles require separate exercise from those normally done for the arm

and shoulders. The first of three exercises that address the rotator cuff muscles will strengthen the external rotators of the upper extremity (infraspinatus and teres minor).

Lie on your side with your head supported and your elbow bent at 90 degrees. Place a folded towel between your elbow and rib cage so that there is a couple of inches between them. Slowly rotate the arm until the weight is pointed upward as far as it is comfortable, then lower the arm slowly back to the starting position. Notice how your palm faces downward during this exercise.

Billy Andrade

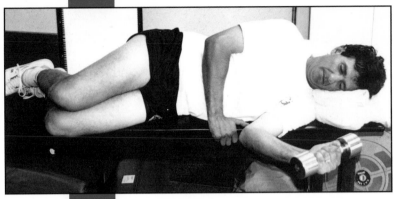

5. Shoulder Internal Rotation

This exercise is done lying on your side, on the edge of a bed, sofa or padded bench. Support your head with a pillow or two. Let your lower elbow slip over the edge, and slightly out in front of you, and bend it to 90 degrees. While holding the dumbbell, rotate the forearm up to your chest, then return it to the starting position. You will probably be somewhat strong with this move, therefore you should be able to use a heavier weight than you used with the previous rotator cuff exercise.

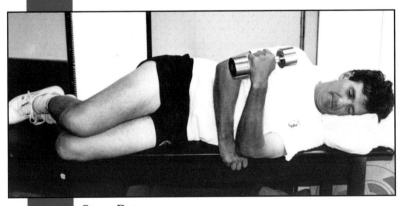

Steve Pate

6. Shoulder Abduction/Flexion/Internal Rotation

This lateral arm raise addresses the supraspinatus muscle in the rotator cuff. Start by holding light weights in your hands with your thumbs turned toward the floor and your arms down. Rather than extending your arms straight out to the side, slowly

raise them slightly forward, in a plane about 30 degrees. Keep your elbows slightly flexed with your thumbs pointed down toward the floor.

Lift your arms to slightly below shoulder level, keeping your body as still as possible.

Then slowly lower your arms to the starting position and repeat. Lifting your arms higher than shoulder level may aggravate the shoulder and will not give you any added benefit.

Fred Couples

45

CHAPTER FOUR

PROGRAM B

Flexibility Program B

1. Lateral Neck Stretch
2. Shoulder Blade Spread
3. Side Lying Trunk Stretch
4. Sitting Knee to Opposite Shoulder
5. Hamstring Stretch
6. Hands/Knees Back Arch and Sag

1. Lateral Neck Stretch

For most golfers, the muscles that extend from the top of the spine and the base of the skull down to the shoulder are invariably tight, and susceptible to soreness, pulls and strains. It is important to stretch this area regularly, especially in a sport that requires so much shoulder activity and twisting of the body around a fixed head.

This stretch is done in a sitting position and addresses the side of the neck and top of the shoulder. Once seated, hang onto the side of the chair with your right hand, then lean away from that arm and drop your left ear to the left shoulder. Hold for 10 - 15 seconds and repeat. Next, repeat on the other side. Hold onto the left edge of the chair and lean to the right so your right ear drops toward the right shoulder.

Jim Colbert

2. Shoulder Blade Spread

This exercise separates the shoulder blades (scapula) from the spine, lengthens the muscles in this hard-to-reach area and eases tension. Golfers have a relatively high incidence of injury here because it is so hard to stretch. Muscles that control the shoulder blade are very active throughout the swing.

While standing, simply grab your shoulder blades as if you were hugging yourself. Drop your chin between your arms and lean forward as you take a deep breath. Hold for a 10 - 15 count and repeat.

Chip Beck

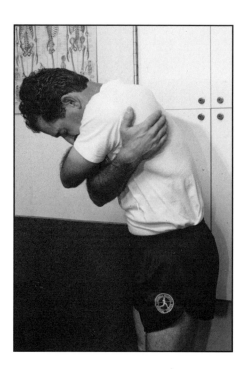

50

3. Side Lying Trunk Rotation Stretch

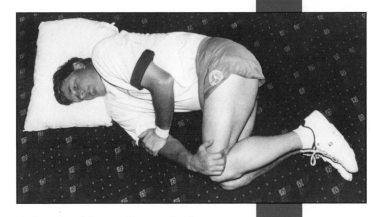

Our studies have shown that the trunk turn is critical in the swing. Greater separation between the hips and the shoulders will stretch the trunk muscles further making them ready to contract quicker and harder, like a stretched rubber band. This exercise will loosen up the spine and muscles in the trunk. Lie on your side on the floor with your knees and hips flexed to 90 degrees.

Place the lower hand on top of your knees. With your upper arm straight, rotate your trunk and arm backwards toward the floor. Make sure that your knees stay together and on the floor. Hold this position for 30

Mike Hill

seconds and repeat this two times. Do the same exercise on the other side. Your goal is, over time, to get your upper back and shoulders as close to the floor as possible.

4. Sitting Knee To Opposite Shoulder

Many golfers have a tight lower back and hip girdle area which restricts their turn. This forces them to use their arms to "muscle" the ball as they swing. Using this particular stretch will elongate the muscles of the hips - including the hip abductors, rotators and gluteus maximus - and minimize the risk of injury.

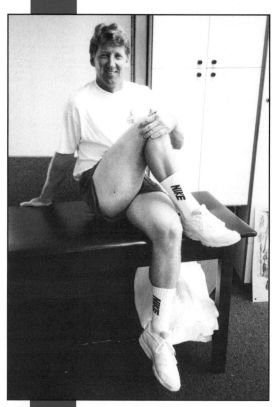

Start by sitting tall on a firm surface. Place your right foot on the other side of your left thigh on the seat. Then grab your right knee with your left hand. Place your right hand behind you. You should receive a stretch in your right hip and buttock when you pull the right knee toward your left shoulder. Hold this stretch for 10 - 15 seconds, then repeat. Switch your position to the other side and do two stretches.

Kenny Knox

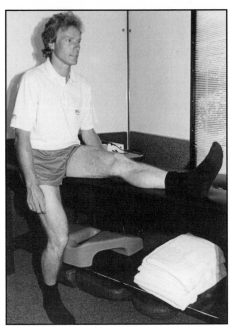

5. Hamstring Stretch

We spend so much time sitting for long periods at work, home and in the car, that the hamstrings become tight. The hamstring muscles will influence movement, and the position of the pelvis and low back. Good flexibility in the hamstrings will allow you to bend forward at the hip and save straining the low back.

Start this stretch by sitting on the side of a firm bed or sofa. Place one foot on the floor and have the other leg laid straight out on the bed. Lean into the straight leg so that you have a comfortable stretch behind the leg. Hold this position for a slow 10 - 15 count, then relax for 10 - 15 seconds, and repeat. Reverse your position and stretch the other leg.

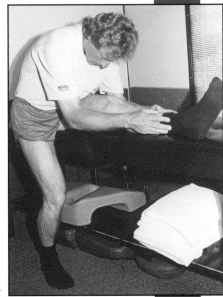

Bernhard Langer

6. Hands/Knees Back Arch and Sag

This spine flexion and extension movement helps loosen up spinal joints. Place yourself on your hands and knees on the floor. Your hands should be underneath your shoulders as much as possible with the elbows straight. The knees are placed directly below the hips. The first movement requires you to push your back up high toward the ceiling in an arching posture. Your shoulder blades should spread and separate from the spine. Let your head drop down in a relaxed position. Hold this position for a 5-count. Then let your back sag to the floor as much as possible. The shoulder blades should pinch together as your head lifts up and backwards. Repeat these two exercises for 10 repetitions.

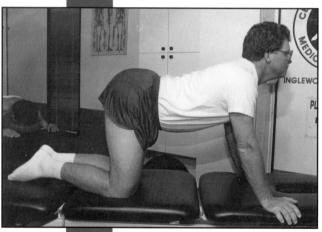

Tom Kite

54

Home Strengthening Program B

1. Chair Squats

2. Hip Abduction/External Rotation

3. Hip Abduction/Internal Rotation

4. Partial Sit-up/Diagonal Sit-up

5. Wrist Flexion

6. Wrist Extension

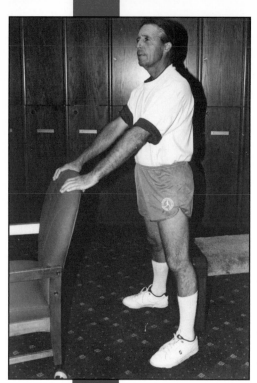

1. Chair Squats

Strong quadriceps (the muscles along the front of the thigh) and the gluteus maximus muscle (the muscle in the buttocks) are very important in golf, helping provide lower body power and stability as you swing. Traditionally most athletes strengthen their "quads" and gluteus maximus by using weight across their shoulders to provide resistance. But you can develop this strength by doing "chair squats," which are easier on the knees and upper back, and more convenient. This exercise is used by players on the pro tour who have had back problems, without aggravating their symptoms.

Using two chairs, hold onto the back of a chair for balance and stability. The chair behind you will keep you from going down too far and help ensure consistency. Starting in an erect position, slowly touch the seat of the chair, maintaining good posture so the

Gary Player

buttocks and quads are doing the work. Place a pillow or several books on the chair if it is too low.

Start by doing 10 repetitions with a two-second pause at the bottom, until you can do three sets of 10 reps with a 5-count hold at the bottom. Fatigue in your thighs means you are working the muscles correctly, but stop if there is pain around your knees. As you become stronger, you can squat lower to gain increased resistance, provided you are balanced and secure. Gradually increase the benefit by holding the squat position for a longer period of time and doing more repetitions. Do not let your buttocks go lower than your knees, as this forces the knees into a vulnerable position.

Remember that technique is especially important here. When done correctly (with the back and pelvis in a neutral position, avoiding a forward or backward tilt in the belt line) this exercise will encourage good posture and give your spine stability and support. Meanwhile, as you improve your strength, you are also improving body balance by working the smaller muscles of the hips.

2. Hip Abduction/External Rotation

We have stressed the importance of the hips and thighs as you rotate in the golf swing and drive

through the ball. During the club take-away to the top of your backswing, your left thigh rotates outward in relation to the pelvis while the right thigh rotates inward. These movements change direction from the top of the swing to the follow-through. Strengthening the muscles that support this motion enables you to turn your hips through the swing more quickly.

Lie on your right side on the floor with your hips flexed to no more than 45 degrees. Your knees should be bent at 90 degrees. The movement to strengthen your hip is to lift your left knee towards the ceiling while keeping your left foot in the starting position. When done correctly you should feel the effort in the left buttock and outside hip. Start by doing 10 repetitions on each side and slowly progress with the recommended increase in sets. To increase the effort to the hip musculature, place a sand bag weight or dumbbell above the knee.

Tommy Aaron

3. Hip Adduction/Internal Rotation

This hip exercise complements the previous one, allowing the inner thigh muscles and the outer hip muscles to work together - just as they should do when you swing a golf club.

Lie on your right side and place your left leg on the seat of a chair or low table. Flex the right hip to 45 degrees and the knee to 90 degrees. You are trying to strengthen the muscles on the inside of the right thigh and hip. Your

movement is to lift the right knee towards the ceiling while keeping your foot on the ground. Repeat this movement 10 times for each leg and gradually increase the sets as suggested. Resistance may be added here by placing a weight above the right knee.

Kermit Zarley

4. Abdominal Crunches

To handle the twisting and turning of a good golf swing, you need to strengthen your abdominals. We recommend the abdominal curl, which differs slightly from the conventional sit-up.

The real payoff from this exercise comes when you add diagonal patterns or crossovers. This strengthens the external and internal "obliques" located along the sides of the abdominal area.

Since the abdominal muscles help counterbalance tightness in the lower back extensors, strengthening your abdominals can help prevent lower-back problems. You will also offset the continuous forward tilt of the pelvis, caused by tight low-back extensors and weak abdominals.

4A. Partial Sit-up

Start by laying on the floor on your back. Bend your knees to a 45 degree angle with your feet flat on the ground. Place your hands behind your neck to help support the head. Raise your shoulders off the floor about 6 - 8 inches. Concentrate on pulling your lower rib cage to your pelvis. Try to keep your neck relaxed and straight. Exhale when you sit-up and inhale when returning to the floor. Perform two sets of 10 - 15 repetitions.

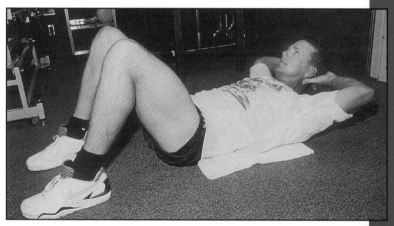

Payne Stewart

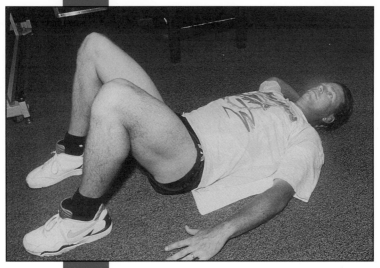

4B. Diagonal Partial Sit-Up

The starting position is the same as the partial sit-up exercise. Place your right hand behind your neck. Leaving your left shoulder and arm on the floor, begin by raising your right shoulder diagonally off the floor approximately 6-8 inches. Exhale when sitting up and inhale when returning to the floor. Perform two sets of 10 - 15 repetitions. Gradually increase to three sets of 10 - 15 repetitions. Reverse the arm positions and repeat to the other side.

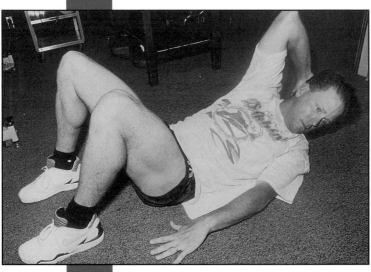

Payne Stewart

The Importance of Strong Hands and Forearms

In her book, *The Complete Golfer*, Nancy Lopez commented that, overall, PGA TOUR pros have better short games than the women pros. "I think a big reason for this is the strength they have in their hands," she wrote. "You need strength to make the delicate little movements that spell the difference between great shotmaking and simply being decent around the greens."

These comments apply to most amateurs, too, who lack strength from the elbow down through the fingertips. Strong forearms, wrists and hands are not only important in a short game, they also provide additional power when you are teeing off, striking the ball from the fairway, or trying to recover from the rough. Furthermore, they help you maintain a firm grip and clubhead stability through impact.

"I exercise my forearms regularly," says Gary Player. "You have to be strong in your hands and arms to play this game well. If you are going to improve, you have to practice, which means hitting a lot of balls. The hands, wrists, and arms take a beating, therefore the stronger you are in that area, the better you'll be."

In a biomechanically sound golf swing, you must transfer energy in a sequence from your legs to your trunk to your shoulders, and out to the club. If the clubhead is wobbling, this energy is dissipated and you won't strike the ball as accurately.

To gain more club control and finesse, as well as prevent hand and wrist injuries, it is important to strengthen this part of your anatomy.

We recommend doing the following exercises to strengthen your hands, wrists and forearms.

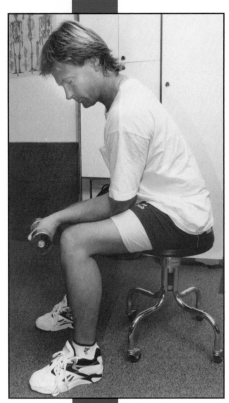

5. Wrist Flexion

Do this exercise while seated, with your forearm supported on a table or on your leg. Your wrist should be over the edge, palm facing up. Lift a weight slowly, flexing the wrist, then lower the weight to the starting position. Work toward three sets of 10 repetitions before switching sides. Think of this routine as "palm up" curls.

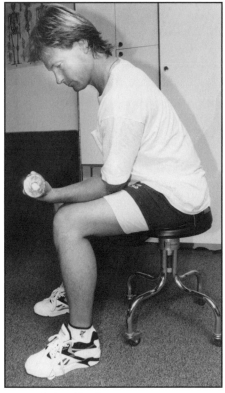

John Cook

6. Wrist Extension

Remain seated, this time with your palm turned toward the floor for "palm down" curls. Keeping your forearm flat against the surface, lift the weight by extending your wrist up as far as you can, then lower it to its original position. Repeat this exercise with the opposite hand and try three sets of 10 repetitions.

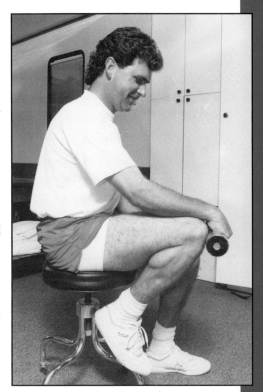

Kelly Gibson

CHAPTER FIVE

FIRST TEE SWING EXERCISES

First Tee Stretches

It is important that you warm up and stretch just before approaching the first tee. The stretches in Program A are designed with that in mind. They can be done in the locker room or out on the course. So, you may want to keep your stretching exercise card from Program A handy in your locker. We can't guarantee it will keep you from miss-hitting your first couple of shots, but you will enhance your chances of starting right. After you have stretched your joints and muscle tissue with the exercises in our Program A, prepare your body for the swing by using a faster, more dynamic routine shortly before teeing off. This exercise will provide a comfortable transition.

You may be wondering, "What's wrong with a 'wedge-to-driver' type of warm-up on the driving range? That's the way some TOUR pros loosen up before playing." True, a wedge-to-driver routine limbers up many of the golf muscles, but it takes a lot of time and does not prepare the lower back for the strain of bending over on the practice putting green, teeing up the ball or fixing ball marks. Nor does it work all the major muscle groups necessary for a full range of motion.

If you tend to be a slow starter in golf, chances are you haven't warmed up and stretched beforehand, forcing your body to perform with an added handicap. Muscles that are warm and stretched prior to teeing off are supple and loose, enabling your body to perform to its full potential. Simply knowing you are warmed up and physically ready to play also gives you greater mental confidence.

1) Trunk Rotation With Club

Stand tall and place your feet together. Place the butt end of the club in the middle of your chest and, with both arms extended out horizontally, grab the shaft of the club. Slowly rotate your body to the left and pause at the end of a comfortable range. Repeat the same motion to the right.

Greg Cesario

Repeat six times in each direction. Twist a little less than full range the first couple of repetitions, then gradually increase the distance you rotate. The key is to feel the rhythm and balance throughout the exercise.

2) Round The Clock

With your feet still together, take your normal grip on the club and bend forward as if addressing the ball. Imagine your club is pointed down to the six o'clock position on the face of a clock.

First, take the club up to the eight o'clock position, then move it forward to the four o'clock position. Repeat this slow and controlled motion four times in each direction.

Greg Cesario

70

Continue taking the club back and forth, from nine to three o'clock several times. Without stopping, increase the range of your swing to a three-quarters backswing and follow-through. Be aware of your tempo and balance throughout this exercise, as it helps with warm-up and golf swing rhythm.

Greg Cesario

3) The "OK" Drill

Greg Cesario

This is the "OK" drill. Start by taking your normal stance and address position. When comfortable, say "OK," then take the club up to the top of the back-swing and stop. Briefly feel and assess this position and again say, "OK." From the top of your back-swing, turn your body, complete the swing and hold that posture. Again, feel and assess your finish, then say "OK," and relax. Repeat this routine three times.

"The benefit of this drill," says teaching golf professional Ron Bakich, "is to realize that the golf swing is really two parts in different directions. The first part is the backward motion to the top, where you stop before changing directions. The second part is the forward motion to the finish. You will establish your own rhythm and realize how crucial balance is in a good swing."

Though this exercise with a club is designed for the first tee and practice range, you can repeat this drill in your home or office. You can also use a yard-stick or a hammer, or nothing at all.

CHAPTER SIX

OTHER FITNESS FACTORS

Cardiovascular/Aerobics Endurance

"You don't realize how important endurance is until you don't have it," says Kenny Knox. "A year or so ago my wife and I were chatting when we suddenly realized that I played well after I'd been working out for awhile. The slumps came when I hadn't. I know that sounds simplistic, but it's true. If you're not tired the last three or four holes of the day or for the last round, you have a lot better chance of winning."

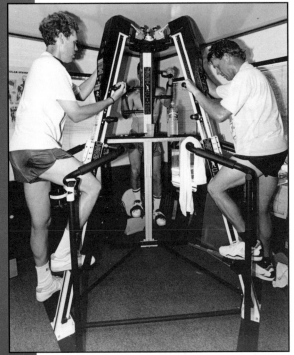

The last component of your total fitness program for golf is cardiovascular endurance. This is done by including 2 - 3 aerobic workouts each week, in a sport or activity that works large muscle groups rhythmically and keeps you breathing hard for at least 20 minutes. Prior to beginning the aerobic activity, it is once again important to stretch. Select an aerobic activity that suits your personality and equipment availability: running, brisk walking, bicycling, swimming, low-impact aerobics, racquetball, stationary bicycling, or rowing on a machine all meet the need of sustained vigorous movement.

Depending upon your fitness level, you need to exercise at 60 to 80 percent of your maximum capacity for more than 20 minutes to elevate your heart rate and give your cardiovascular system a meaningful aerobic workout. (You can roughly calculate your maximum heart rate by subtracting your age from 220. Then multiply that number by .60, .70 or .80 to gain a target heart rate level at which to exercise.) If you are just beginning an aerobic program, start at the lower level of 60 percent. Gradually increase the workload to a rate that is relatively comfortable yet pushes you toward your ultimate goal of 80 percent. If you have had any cardiovascular problems, check with your physician.

While walking and playing golf will not meet these aerobic requirements (even if you are walking quickly from one shot to the next) you shouldn't underrate its benefits. You can cover at least four to five miles while playing a round of golf, and it will enhance your endurance, leg strength and muscle tone. As our colleague, Robert K. Kerlan, M.D., has pointed out, "The golfer who rides a cart may be shooting a great game, but he is ruining a good walk in the process."

Even if you don't have the time or the inclination to add a vigorous aerobic activity to your weekly routine, at least incorporate more walking into your daily schedule. Walking 30 minutes in your neighborhood several times a week will improve your endurance on the golf course, especially if you work up to a brisk pace.

Not only does you body benefit from aerobic conditioning, your golf game will too. Greater muscle endurance and less fatigue - the by-products of aerobic fitness - will lead to improved stroking consistency. You'll feel improved stamina in adjusting to long or hilly courses, coping with hot weather, or simply playing better during the final holes of a close match. Greater stamina will also enhance your enjoyment of the sport. Senior

TOUR player, and exercise enthusiast, Bob Charles, exercises on the stationary bike three to five times a week for a half hour each time. "It is important for me to keep my cardiovascular system in shape," reports Bob. "Since I prefer to walk the golf course, I need to keep my legs in shape. With the exercise program, I don't get tired anymore."

In summary, you will increase your overall enjoyment of golf as you improve your physical condition. By getting in shape - and maintaining that condition - you will also gain a competitive edge and decrease your risk of injury.

Golf Related Injuries

While golf may not be an overly taxing game for many club players, injuries still occur. We are finding that the most common injuries and complaints are in the lower back and between the shoulder blades, high in the back, and near the base of the neck. In golf, the susceptibility to these problems comes with the territory. Every time you swing a club, you are rotating your entire spine while attempting to keep your head still and bent slightly forward in the address position. Using our exercises regularly to stretch and strengthen the neck, trunk and lower back will help offset these potential problems so you can swing pain-free all season.

Another source of golf injuries is too much of a good thing, not only on the pro tour but among club players everywhere. This "overuse syndrome" contributes to injuries in two ways.

First, a player can overuse golf muscles simply by hitting too many balls on the driving range, day after day. When you consider that a pro golfer averages anywhere from 150 to 300 swings a day — on the course and at the practice range — it is easy to see how injuries crop up, especially early degenerative problems from using the neck and lower back too much. True, practice is essential on the tour, but when coupled with 18 holes of golf nearly every day, eventually something is likely to weaken. Fortunately, when the pros condition and train their soft tissue with a moderate exercise program like ours, they find they can tolerate this undue stress.

You may be thinking, "That sounds logical, but doesn't it only apply to the pro game?" Not necessarily. Should you decide to take the game more seriously — practicing more often and hitting more golf balls — your body's vulnerable areas are susceptible to the overuse syndrome. Use good sense. If you want to improve your swing, but are not yet in good shape, avoid doing too much  for too long, especially on the driving range.

Another problem is that many club players "pound" balls, using questionable mechanics to the point that practice becomes harmful. Constant swinging puts additional strain on the body, and can eventually lead to injury. Studies conducted at Centinela Hospital's Biomechanics Laboratory have shown that professional golfers activate the same muscles each time they swing, resulting in a consistent, desirable stroke. In contrast, amateurs have erratic muscle control, and often cannot duplicate shot after shot.

Generally, there is a limit to what you can accomplish by practicing, with a fine line of diminishing returns. If you let common sense prevail, you will realize when the time and effort invested in practice are no longer producing the desired results. If you should suffer an injury and are forced to discontinue play, follow your doctor's advice.

Guidelines For Good Body Mechanics And Safeguarding The Back

This golf exercise program will help you avoid golf-related injuries if you don't overlook sensible body mechanics, particularly involving the lower back.

A

Mike Sullivan (incorrect)

Most back injuries, in fact, are not solely attributed to poor golf swing mechanics. They are compounded by improper body mechanics when teeing the ball, removing it from the cup, or during prolonged practice. All three of these activities involve bending forward at the waist. This forward bending dramatically increases the pressure in the intervertebral disks of the lower back.

Here are some suggestions to help you avoid these back problems:

1. Always be careful when you pick up your bag, whether you are loading it in the car, lifting it out of the trunk, or picking it up after every shot during play. The bag is heavy and cumbersome, and bending over to pick it up from an awkward standing position (Photo A) imposes tremendous strain on the spine.

Be especially careful if you are leaving for the course early in the morning or arriving there after a lengthy drive, since your body is still stiff and even more vulnerable to injury.

Notice in Photos B and C how your body should be positioned as you load and unload your bag from a car. Instead of jerking the bag, bend at the knees and make sure your lower back is slightly arched for greater leverage. Remember to use good body posture and common sense even if you feel strong and healthy.

C

Mike Sullivan
(correct)

A   *Tom Sieckman (incorrect)*

2. Make sure you are bending down properly when teeing up your ball, repairing divot marks on the green, or removing the ball from the cup. Do not bend over at the waist without bending the knees (Photo A). For added back support, always bend the knees and try to use your club (Photo B). This is the safest method if you have a back problem. Another method would be that of the golfer in Photo C, who is using his right hand to tee up with his left hand on the golf club for balance. He has a slight flex in the right leg as his left leg extends back in the air. Raising your leg up behind you means that you are flexing at the hip joint, not in the lower back.

B

3. When practicing on the putting green, take frequent breaks to stand erect and arch your back. A good preventative exercise is to stop periodically and do a standing back bend to counter all the forward bending you are doing as you putt. Otherwise,

cramping muscle pains may occur when you hold a rigid, bentover body position for an extended period, hitting one putt after another.

Poor posture is a frequent cause of back disorders, so pay close attention to the way you carry your body as you play a round of golf. The golf swing can make you rounded in the shoulders, and when you assume that position week after week, the tendency is to maintain it even when you are not swinging. So hold a good posture when you're between shots.

Tom Sieckman (correct)

C

A helpful hint is to think and stand tall. This puts many body structures in a neutral, decompressed position.

These tips should help keep you from developing low back pain and related problems in the years ahead - specifically by reducing lumbar intervertebral disk pressure.

Using Your Good Judgement

There is the old adage that "Practice makes Perfect," and oh, how we know that to be true. Research done in our Biomechanics Laboratory has shown us that professional athletes have a very precise and very consistent pattern of exactly how they use their muscles. On the other hand, people who are learning the sport demonstrate a nonspecific muscle activation pattern as well as inconsistent performance. And, the only way to move from a nonspecific to a precise muscle pattern is practice-practice-practice.

But practice-practice-practice must be balanced with rest from the activity. Too much practice can lead to overuse of the tissues, microtrauma and ultimately injury.

We have found that the most common area of injury in golfers is in the back. This makes sense as you think of the extreme trunk rotation used for each golf swing and multiply that by however many swings it takes you to play a round of golf (and don't forget to add in your efforts at the driving range). A pro golfer averages anywhere between 150 - 300 swings a day; and that is an efficient golfer! Fortunately, when the pros condition and train with an exercise program such as the one in this book, the risk to the tissues is minimized, injury is avoided and they can continue to play their game.

The message to you is to use your judgement. Rather than doing too much for too long, choose to gradually get in shape. By combining your good judgement with the three components of being in shape (flexibility, strength, and endurance), you can excel and enjoy your love for golf.

Frank W. Jobe

Frank Wilson Jobe, M.D., is a co-founder and president of the Kerlan-Jobe Orthopaedic Clinic and Medical Director of the Biomechanics Research Laboratory at Centinela Hospital Medical Center. He is the orthopaedic consultant for the Los Angeles Dodgers Baseball Team and orthopaedic consultant to the PGA TOUR. In addition, he is Clinical Professor of Orthopaedics at the University of Southern California, School of Medicine. He has authored over 100 medical articles and has given hundreds of lectures on orthopaedics and sports medicine.

Lewis A. Yocum

Lewis A. Yocum, M.D., is also an orthopaedic consultant to the PGA TOUR, and associate medical director of Centinela Hospital's Biomechanics Laboratory. In addition, he is the orthopaedic consultant for the California Angels, physician to the Lewitzky Dance Company,and consultant to Centinela Hospital's Fitness Institute. Dr. Yocum is an orthopaedic and sports medicine specialist at the Kerlan-Jobe Orthopedic Clinic in Inglewood, California. He is also Clinical Assistant Professor in Orthopaedics at the University of Southern California. He has published numerous articles and lectured extensively in this field.

Robert E. Mottram

Robert E. Mottram, PT, ATC, is a Registered Physical Therapist, Certified Athletic Trainer, and a clinical specialist in athletic rehabilitation.

His background and expertise in golf span 15 years. He has been treating and exercising professional golfers from the PGA TOUR, Senior PGA TOUR, and LPGA TOUR for seven years. He presently writes health and fitness articles for golf instructional magazines.

Marilyn M. Pink

Marilyn M. Pink, MS, PT, is the director of the Biomechanics Research Laboratory at Centinela Hospital Medical Center. For eleven years, she has combined her backgrounds of Physical Therapy, Biomechanics and Biometry in order to understand, optimize and rehabilitate Olympic and professional athletes. She has published over 60 professional articles, has won numerous research awards and has lectured internationally.

Centinela Hospital Medical Center

Centinela Hospital Medical Center, based in Inglewood, California, is the official hospital and medical research center of the PGA TOUR and Senior PGA TOUR. Combining this experience with ongoing research in its Biomechanics Laboratory, Centinela Hospital has become a valuable source of expert information for golfers at all levels.

FLEXIBILITY PROGRAM A

 1. Neck Rotation

 2. Posterior Shoulder Stretch

 3. Chest Stretch

 4. Trunk Forward Flexion

 5. Trunk Rotation

 6. Trunk Side Bend Stretch

FLEXIBILITY
PROGRAM B

 1. Lateral Neck Stretch

 2. Shoulder Blade Spread

 3. Side Lying Trunk Stretch

 4. Sitting Knee to Opposite
Shoulder

 5. Hamstring Stretch

 6. Hands/Knees Back Arch
and Sag

STRENGTHENING PROGRAM A

 1. Countertop Push-ups with a Plus

 2. Bent-over Row

 3. Shoulder Extension

 4. Shoulder External Rotation

 5. Shoulder Internal Rotation

 6. Shoulder Abduction/ Flexion/Internal Rotation

STRENGTHENING

STRENGTHENING
PROGRAM B

 1. Chair Squats

 2. Hip Abduction/External Rotation

 3. Hip Abduction/Internal Rotation

 4. Partial Sit-up

 5. Diagonal Sit-up

 6. Wrist Flexion

 7. Wrist Extension